Witness Marks

poems by

Andrew Szilvasy

Finishing Line Press
Georgetown, Kentucky

Witness Marks

Copyright © 2020 by Andrew Szilvasy
ISBN 978-1-64662-359-4 First Edition
All rights reserved under International and Pan-American Copyright Conventions. No part of this book may be reproduced in any manner whatsoever without written permission from the publisher, except in the case of brief quotations embodied in critical articles and reviews.

ACKNOWLEDGMENTS

"Witness Marks" first appeared in *CutBank*
"After School is Out" first appeared in *Cease, Cows*
Both "Anecdotes" and "Easter in Portsmouth" first appeared in *Typehouse*
"Strangers" first appeared in *The Moth*
"Epistle" first appeared in *Alabama Literary Review*
"Snake Lips" first appeared in *Dunes Review*
"Convalescence" first appeared in *WestWard Quarterly*
"Photorealism" first appeared in *Dime Show Review*
"Whirlwind" first appeared in the *American Journal of Poetry*
"Haircut before Funeral" first appeared in *Carve*
"Burying the Cat" first appeared in *Modern Poetry Quarterly Review*
"Severed" first appeared in *Barrow Street*
"While the Foliage Sleeps" first appeared in *Fourth & Sycamore*
"Winter Psalm" first appeared in *Plainsongs*
"Beyond All Change" first appeared in *Loch Raven Review*

Publisher: Leah Huete de Maines
Editor: Christen Kincaid
Cover Art: *Green Door* by Abbie Wanamaker
Author Photo: Paula Guzmán
Cover Design: Elizabeth Maines McCleavy

Order online: www.finishinglinepress.com
also available on amazon.com

Author inquiries and mail orders:
Finishing Line Press
P. O. Box 1626
Georgetown, Kentucky 40324
U. S. A.

Table of Contents

Witness Marks 1

After School Is Out 2

Strangers 3

Anecdotes 4

Epistle 6

Snake Lips 8

Convalescence 9

Photorealism 10

Whirlwind 11

[The opalescent droplet] 12

Haircut before Funeral 13

Burying the Cat 14

Digging a Hole 15

Easter in Portsmouth 16

Memories of Your Face 17

Severed 18

While the Foliage Sleeps 19

[The sphere has cracked] 20

Winter Psalm 21

Beyond All Change 22

Witness Marks

Before he died, my father left the carcass
      of a birds-eye maple table
in the basement, witness marks all laid out
      for a drop leaf when the cancer

came, smoothing the round edge of his paunch
      with its hand plane. Deathgray, the fat
man began to hate the smell of thyme
      and onion, the texture of scallops.

When my mother moved, we used it as a bier,
      one leg missing and the top
barely proud of the apron, to remove
      the last awls and adzes from

the cellar, bore them all up those long steps
      to the cold light and set them
on our old sidewalk to wait for a stranger
      who might never show up.

After School Is Out

and the run through the pink clouds has
ended, he skulks up the stairs and crosses
the threshold into the dark living room. Sweat

runs down his nose and falls onto the amaranth
tiles designed to camouflage the mud

and keep it from the phony hardwood floor.
On the couch a man watches a Mets game
and a woman beside him smokes Newports.

She eats a Hungry Man dinner in the TV light.
The man owned a sports bar years ago, and on that

old bar top still there are dozens of baseball
cards with his thin face pasted over the players',
all smiling beneath thirty years of varnish.

Strangers

When he first noticed he was losing weight
Dad joked he was a stranger in a strange land

where it didn't matter what he ate
his body would continue losing weight.

Of course, this was before the radiation,
before the wheelchair and slender hands,

just months from noticing he was losing weight,
before he was a stranger in stranger lands.

Anecdotes

    That summer, Uncle Billy got himself
                in trouble again,
       (he seemed to bear the mark of Cain)
     and moved into our dollhouse, space
          so scant we felt our limbs
          forced out of its windows.
We sensed each other's heartbeats in our arms.

And every day he'd piss my mother off:
                she was certain
    he wasn't working, that she smelled gin,
    and she believed she saw the men
        that he was hiding from.
           He wouldn't hear her fears,
and yet he wore a hat for many years.

It wasn't just the arguments that kept them
                at each others' throats.
    Good God that heat spurs anecdotes
    still at get-togethers: paint
        bubbled off the walls,
        heat haze emanated
from our warped metal appliances. Our house

smelled always: musk and mildew paired with rotten
                chicken soup.
    The freezer labored to meet ice cube
    demand, complaining constantly
        with this high pitched hum.
        It's a damn wonder we
still talk at all. And then one night it peaks:

my mother shrieks, and dad runs out
                    of one room Bill
          another, and he's swinging like a windmill
       a bat above his battered hair.
                Eyes intent, buck-
             naked but for cowboy
boots and tattoos, he sees this fluff and screams,

high-stepping circles—dancing with a mouse.
                    Dad and I
      roar and glance at Mom, who's red-eyed.
      We're just sure she's going to cuss—
             but she doubles over with
                a laugh that even now
can reach into the cracks of any room.

Epistle
To Brett, on the Death of his Mother

You know, old friend, this moment stands too large
for speech, plus I don't have the gear for dirge:
it's happiness or philosophical
reflections free from much emotional
heft always, and I'm many miles away,
at that, writing from a Jordaan café.
And there can be no real condolences
when one's mother walks among the shades:
it's ancient water smashing at chalk cliffs
that tear not just the rock but also rip
the very breath out of our throats. You sense
Poseidon has been slighted by offenses
you inadvertently made, and now he crafts
bronze cruelties, pours into their hollow casts—

But it's just silence. Leaves fall off the trees
even when the air is still. It feels
like only Everest stands unburied but
we know that too will be filed down to dust.
Our life is dew and this world's core is fire
coolly boiling off what we admire.

I wish that I could offer you my prayers
but they'd mean nothing to the man upstairs
  after all my years of benign negligence.
  But let me offer you these few words without the pretense
they carry with them metaphysical
comfort or anything too mystical.

So look, you never do get over it,
though after time forced smiles you counterfeit
for others morph into rough facsimiles
of happiness, and then eventually
you're back, more or less, as Hemingway
would say, stronger in these broken places.

You can't unsee your wasted mother lying
a monument to ephemerality
inside a box you didn't know she bought:
that sight will never really leave your thoughts,
but in this moment shines more brightly than
all other memories, as if the sun
exploded in your mind and littered it
with light down to your reptile brain's gill-slits:
so thoroughly death colors everything.
      Yet when it dims
there's space for all those background stars to trim
the newly darkened sky, although their light
will always have a melancholy tint.
It's like how snow-topped mountains bring a coolness
despite their peaks residing in the distance.

Though I'm an atheist, Qohelet
brought me some solace: sun rising and sun setting,
all that. And Matthew, too: the Father "sendeth
rain on the just and on the unjust." Sound
sense, though that fatalism only works
in even hours. At odd hours I was sure
      crickets deserved blame
      whenever darkness came.

Regardless, I hope you find at least a spoonful
of what meager comfort's possible.
    If you were over here as planned,
      I'd buy you a drink. The offer stands
when I get back to your neck of town.
Drinks are all I'm good for, as you know.

Snake Lips

                Under the lone stone, the eel
                      hid from the white light.
    Tempted, maybe, by the fiddler
                          crab, body-
        sized orange claw held out like

                Hector when outside
the walls he begged for life. The eel
                      sat quiet, no
      pitched fight or fast strike for our
              eyes. But floating scraps

the morning after gave such joy
                  to boys still
      eager for some war. Better
           yet, the albino
red snake down the block with pink eyes

                    and orange
      skin was ready to be fed.
                This white mouse had eyes
pink as the snake's, but mammal sight
                    could not help

      it up the glass. All pets are
              imposters: the orange
tabby that purrs in your pink lap,
                  eyes a dis-
      tant bird, and pierces your leg.

Convalescence

The western pave was all aflame
with firewheel petals munched by deer.
An octogenarian dame
waits for an old chevalier
beside a terra cotta bird
bath. A spotted starling soaks its wings
then dashes woods-ward having heard
the grate of a rusty swing
in a fenced-off park.

                        Here the brier
skirts the lot's edges while the woman
sits alone, entwining hand in hair.
Then, by the entrance, a young man
stops, and leaves, staring but a moment
at an oak that rots heartwood out.

Photorealism

          There is this photo
              of Marianne Moore
                  beside
a pony in Greenwich Village
              that like a
      nun fingering beads I thumb
                     to at odd hours

       to contemplate her
              wide smile not yet set
                    beneath
the trifold hat, but imprisoned
             only by
      those hard enjambments and
                    her mother, whom

      Bishop loathed. But no
             matter how much I
             want to
pity her that smile reminds me
            only that
     we make our own prisons
                 and then love them.

Whirlwind

Iodoform, wind rolling,
letters, cards, yellow light.
IV bag, morphine, rattling
through the night.

Sudden gasp. Cricket chirps.
Dirty sheets, still chest,
salt, empty bed, hearse
turning left.

Minister, mortician, tailor.
Mother, sister, brother, niece.
Ashes, urn. Pen, paper—
barren leaves.

Glasses, passport, wallet, license,
type-c prints, wedding ring.
Salt. Water. Water. Silence,
the soul's spring.

[The opalescent droplet]

The opalescent droplet
rarely catches light.
How business-like it merges—
the puddle—filled with quiet.

Haircut before Funeral

My hair is not its usual self: it doesn't
scramble down my ears or snake its way
into the chimney of bone and cartilage.

The tight cut tumbles slower than it should.
She gabs and trims; I imagine worlds
where dirty blonde wisps veil roads like snow.

Burying the Cat

It's rough digging, the roots and rocks halt
the spade, and I'm reminded of the "joke"
the nosy old neighbor told me oh now three times:
"See now that's why they call it West *Rocks*-bury!"

Her husband, but blind bones now, told her that.
In a cardboard box beside us stuffed with
grave goods (toys, her food bowl) she stiffens and
we feel sad and silly, adults mourning a cat.

A cliché, the torrent makes November
that much colder and the squelch that much
louder. These dumb rocks—rocks I toss
among the dying grass only to bury

again, like a dragon hoarding gold, rocks
that as a child I'd gather in July
to blind some giant pond, or if it still could see,
make its pupil dilate, shatter all the dark.

Digging a Hole

Too slender and skin-deep,
pinprick in our playfield;
along the event horizon
you taste the weight of absence.

Easter in Portsmouth

                    Someone's blood bug-
         splattered on my windshield, its form
              fused with wings and fly-eyes
into an elemental paste so thick
                  that water won't

     cleanse the glass. Today the city's
         all but empty. We do
this, we do that, but the shops are locked and
                the wine bar with
    the longed-for Rhône is closed.

          All this loveliness is
starved: its cobbles stripped of steps, these grey waves
               lap a concrete
    wall stained a tepid green, as if
          even the sea were half-

hearted. Beside a dumpster there's a bar
               with a view: one
    kayaker in a red drysuit
          paddles among rusted
tugboats. We pour the wine but taste the blood.

Memories of Your Face

A curious gestalt:
like ripples on the water,

heat-haze over asphalt.
Like God among the slaughter.

Severed

The widow brings her neighbors fresh-cut flowers,
the same rhododendron blossoms she forgot
she brought them yesterday. They'll bloom among

the watermelon rinds and chicken bones
fitfully dragged to curbs in body bags,
now more purple and more sweetly scented.

While the Foliage Sleeps

For you, the visit balms the loss. He'll lurk
in our old house, miscolored now, where once
out back in the beige yard he scorched the stump

to ash, and you, five, cried while termites burned.
Perhaps he's at your wedding now, the one
you thought that he had missed (*who was*

it now that walked you down the darkened aisle?),
yet there he stands cool against the copper sky.
Sometimes his clothes are dripping, his blazer's tight

at the shoulders, but he smells right, and the size
of his pupils, black disks of dark—the whole
of his eye!—while strange, makes sense. The mind adjusts.

But my dream-soaked father never stays
with me. Always, walking out of oceans
or just amid the normal conversations

while falling down the gulches, just when his lips
begin to mouth the things I wish they would
my sense returns, and even if he lingers

I wake, and headlights—luminous spiders—crawl
up the wall and vanish into corners of the dark.

[The Sphere has cracked]

The Sphere has cracked. Mere eye contact.
You brood about the sky.
Everything is far more brittle
than you thought it'd be.

Winter Psalm

The wheezing sun glints
    a nuthatch gathers plastic holly.
A silver tabby stares from the snow.
    The neighbor's boy walks his golden retriever.
Across the street a black-hatted figure glowers,
    his scarf flutters where a heart should be.
It means little to this one without gloves,
    his jacket buttons material for fire.

For the man born in winter is of winter,
    he cannot live to spring.
Though he can imagine a fall,
    summer is beyond him.
New Year, let him endure rawness with wisdom.
    Let him feel the peace that comes with knowing
that a man was rolled out of snow,
    that the dog descended from a wolf.

Beyond All Change

The earth is beautiful beyond all change.
I think it's the all that really gets me.
Naked trees in a milk-white field

or eagles picture-still on mountains
that cradle the jaws of late leviathans:
these are beautiful beyond all change.

And I can even see the deep-sea beauty
of the anglerfish, whose
take on love makes true the human lie:

flesh of our flesh, blood of our blood.
But is the poet right about all change?
There will come a time when the bloated

sun will drink the rocks
and breathe the oceans: when we sit
with crows in flaming trees,

will we walk hand-in hand admiring
the mountains that melt around us?

Andrew teaches English outside of Boston and has poems appearing *CutBank, Barrow Street, Smartish Pace, Tar River Poetry, The Moth,* and *RHINO,* among others. Additionally, he was a finalist for the Erskine J. Poetry Prize. He lives in Boston with his wife.

www.ingramcontent.com/pod-product-compliance
Lightning Source LLC
LaVergne TN
LVHW041525070426
835507LV00013B/1819